Financial BARRIERS

Dennis Burke

Dennis Burke Publications

Breaking Financial Barriers
ISBN 1-890026-04-2
© 1997 by Dennis Burke Publications
P. O. Box 150043
Arlington, TX 76015

Unless otherwise indicated, all Scripture
quotations are taken from the *New King
James Version* of the Bible.

Cover design by:
Brian Torvik Design
12029 Stevens Drive
Fort Worth, TX 76126
(817) 249-0342

Dedication

Vikki and I, as well as our staff, would like to express our appreciation to our faithful Partners for joining with us in proclaiming the gospel to hurting people around the world.

Table of Contents

Chapter 1

Breaking
Financial Barriers

For years, it was believed that no one would ever run one mile in under four minutes. Many had tried, but failed. Most believed that the human body could not be developed to break that barrier.

Roger Bannister, however, was different. He didn't let that barrier stop him. He was so convinced it could be done that he continued to push the limits. On May 6, 1954, it happened—at the age of 25, Roger Bannister beat the clock and made history. He proved that the human body could withstand the pace and run one mile in under four minutes. Soon afterward, many others broke the barrier once believed impossible.

Like the four minute mile, the sound barrier seemed like an impenetrable wall. When a pilot came close to the speed of sound, his airplane began to shake so violently he thought it would disintegrate. Then, on October 14, 1947, Chuck Yeager stepped into an X-1 and once again history was made. Although it was a rough ride up to the sound barrier, he found a smooth and quiet ride on the other side.

There has been a similar barrier erected against the Body of Christ. It is a barrier designed to contain and prevent believers from moving into the magnitude of strength and victory Jesus made available. These limitations can affect every area of a Christian's life. I call it the *battle of containment.* Satan erects barriers that are designed to stop you and keep you from advancing in life.

One of the barriers the enemy erects is in the area of finances. We receive prayer requests from all over the world, and one of the most frequent requests we receive is in the area of finances. Financial pressure is one of the major causes of strain in marriage, distress in families and frustration in many of God's people. God's Word instructs believers how to overcome pressure and break down the barriers of lack.

The Promise of No Lack

As God led the children of Israel

through the wilderness, He spoke to them in detail about the promised land. In Deuteronomy 8:9, He said, "A land in which you will eat bread without scarcity, in which you will lack nothing." This land was a place where there would be abundance—lack would be conquered.

God's plan for believers is revealed through His promises. He has promised you just what He promised the children of Israel—you will lack nothing!

As Israel began the transition from life in the wilderness to the land promised to Abraham, God instructed Joshua regarding what he must do to prosper.

No man shall be able to stand before you all the days of your life; as I was with Moses, so I will be with you. I will not leave you nor forsake you. Be strong and of good courage, for to this people you shall divide as an inheritance the land which I swore to their fathers to give them. Only be strong and very courageous, that you may observe to do according to all the law which Moses My servant commanded you; do not turn from it to the right hand or to the left, that you may prosper wherever you go. This Book of the Law shall not depart from your mouth, but you shall meditate in it day and night, that you may observe to do according to all that is written in it. For then you will make your way prosperous, and then you will have good success (Joshua 1:5-8).

God said be strong, be courageous and observe all that is written. Their success was determined, not by God alone, but by their obedience to God's instructions. He said they must meditate in the Word and keep it in their mouth.

Seek First God's Kingdom

Jesus made a powerful statement about the effect your priorities have on material success. "But seek first the kingdom of God and His righteousness, and all these things shall be added to you" (Matthew 6:33).

Your first priority must be to seek God and His ways, then you will be in position to see His power released. God always expects your priorities to be His priorities. Then, all of the *things* can be added to you. The things are not the problem, God wants you to have things. The point He is making is that proper order of your priorities must be maintained.

You must also continue to say what the Word says about your present situation, your past and your future. By doing so, you literally begin to activate the plan of God for your life—increase and abundance! Through diligent application of the laws of God, *you* make your way prosperous.

A prosperous life comes only after your total commitment and obedience to God. There can be no real success while living in disobedience. Your soul must prosper, then you can prosper in all other areas. "Beloved, I pray that you may prosper in all things and be in health, just as your soul prospers" (3 John 2). Before any other part of your life can increase, your spiritual life must prosper. By meditating in the Word and guarding it in your heart, your inner life will flourish. Prosperity flows from the inside out. Your ways must become God's ways and your thoughts like His thoughts.

Your first priority in life is to increase in your relationship with God. Your second priority is to your personal self-esteem. It is hard to obtain and to maintain a break-through if you do not see yourself in the light of God's Word. Your third priority is to prosper in your family relationships. It is vitally important to maintain these priorities if other areas of your life are to increase.

The Counsel of the Ungodly

God wants you to prosper in all things including the material realm.

Psalm 1:1-3 reveals how you must view things in order to see barriers removed.

Blessed is the man who walks not in the counsel of the ungodly, nor stands in the path of sinners, nor sits in the seat of the scornful; but his delight is in the law of the Lord, and in His law he meditates day and night. He shall be like a tree planted by the rivers of water, that brings forth its fruit in its season, whose leaf also shall not wither; and whatever he does shall prosper.

15

The people you surround yourself with reveal a great deal about you. Even though God may use you to minister to those who do not know how to live a victorious life, you must have relationships with those who make deposits into your life. You need the supply of others who will stretch your capacity for increase.

If you embrace the counsel of those who do not have a close relationship with God, you start down a path you really do not want to travel. The influence of those who live in unbelief or strife *will* have an effect on you.

Walking in the Counsel of God

When I first realized I was called to the ministry, I became a youth minister at a powerful church in southern California. I knew then I was called to travel like I do today, but I had to be faithful to do what was at hand. One day a well respected man in the church gave me some fatherly advice. He said, "Dennis, we don't need any more preachers. What God needs is businessmen who will give great sums of money into the work of the kingdom."

I knew he was right, we do need many who will give finances into the ministry, but I also knew that God had called *me* into ministry. The counsel was sincere, but it was sincerely wrong. Ungodly counsel does not necessarily come from ungodly people. This man loved me and wanted me to be as successful as he was. From his point of view, to be a success I needed to do what he had done. But had I taken that counsel, I would have missed the mark. God could not have blessed my efforts because I would have been aiming at second best.

Delight in Him

When you delight in God's Word and His counsel, you keep His plan in your heart. With His plan in your heart, His Word is evident in your mind and conversation. As Psalm 1 said, you will be planted—with the roots of your life reaching deep into His resources—keeping you firmly established in His will. Let the Holy Spirit open your heart to see if you are tolerating a barrier in your life. Disobedience can be a barrier. Disharmony is another barrier. If you give Satan an opportunity, he will take it and use it against you. Allow the Holy Spirit to change your attitude, then begin to sow the seed that will create God's best.

Sow Your Seed for a Result

In the kingdom of God, the law of sowing and reaping reaches into all aspects of life. In order to destroy the barriers that withhold your increase, you must sow seed that will create the harvest you desire. Anything you have can be a seed—your time, your love, your work, your money—anything can be sown into the field of God's kingdom. Whatever seed you sow, when sown in faith, will crush the barriers of the enemy and set your increase in motion. Times of increase and harvest begin as you break the barriers that most consider impossible.

Chapter 2

Our Covenant of Increase

For unto us a Child is born, unto us a Son is given; and the government will be upon His shoulder. And His name will be called Wonderful, Counselor, Mighty God, Everlasting Father, Prince of Peace. Of the increase of His government and peace there will be no end (Isaiah 9:6-7).

To the person who understands the idea of covenant, it is no mystery that the new covenant brings all the blessings of God into the life of the believer. It placed you into a position to receive all of God's goodness and provision.

This covenant brought the two parties together and gave us access into one another's wealth and influence. We had nothing really to offer God, but He had everything to offer us. We received His strength and richness, and He took our weakness and lack.

As the focus of God's love, you have been brought into this covenant by simple faith in the sacrifice of Jesus and have been given the right to receive all that this covenant includes.

It is important to realize that we must provide the avenues for God to bring His plan to us. He is the source of the provision and miracles, but your obedience, your faith and your faithfulness to Him are the pathways that bring His abundance to you.

The more you understand how God thinks about you, the easier it is to be obedient and stand in faith on His Word. Psalm 115 gives us powerful insight into the way He thinks:

> The Lord has been mindful of us; He will bless us; He will bless the house of Israel; He will bless the house of Aaron. He will bless those who fear the Lord, both small and great. May the Lord give you increase more and more, you and your children. May you be blessed by the Lord, Who made heaven and earth. The heaven, even the heavens, are the Lord's; but the earth He has given to

the children of men (verses 12-16).

God's thoughts are fixed on you! He has remembered you. He has not forgotten you or the things you are facing. God is looking for ways to bring His best and His increase into your life. Those verses tell us that God is mindful of us and He has increase on His mind. He is the giver of all good things, and He is moving to bring that increase to you.

Every good gift and every perfect gift is from above, and comes down from the Father of lights, with whom there is no variation or shadow of turning (James 1:17).

He Will Bless You

Whenever we speak about covenants, we must always look back to the covenant between God and Abram.

One of the first things God spoke to Abram was: "I will bless you." These words have been at the very heart of God's desire for all men and women. He is a giver and is committed to bringing His blessings to His people. In establishing a covenant with Abram, God clearly stated what He would bring to him through this agreement. Notice Genesis 12:1-3:

Now the Lord had said to Abram: "Get out of your country, from your family and from your father's house, to a land that I will show you. I will make you a great nation; I will bless you and make your name great; and you shall be a blessing. I will bless those who bless you, and I will curse him who curses you; and in you all the families of the earth shall be blessed."

The Amplified Bible says it this way: "I will make of you a great nation, and I will bless you [with abundant increase of favors]..." He *wants* to bless and favor you.

Abundant Increase

Think about that: abundant increase of the favor of God. God considered it such a priority for His blessings and increase to be brought to mankind, He declared that it was the first thing He would do for Abram—if he would only obey Him.

As Abram began to obey God and to

walk with Him, he saw the power of God's covenant in action. Immediately he would see the increase which it brought him. In Genesis 13:6, it tells of the abundance that Abram and his nephew, Lot, received from the Lord:

> Now the land was not able to support them, that they might dwell together, for their possessions were so great that they could not dwell together.

Their *possessions* had increased abundantly. It was more than they could contain as long as they stayed together. If Abram was to continue to increase, he would need to go on with God and be separated from Lot.

The covenant brought an increase of possessions. But there would be more, God would give him land as far as his eyes could see. He would give Abram descendants, land and increase of wealth as well as influence, all because he would continue to live by faith in the covenant between himself and God Almighty.

God and Abraham...God and You

Abram is called the father of faith. He walked in the kind of faith that is a model to all generations—the faith that pleased God. He believed that his covenant with God would bring him increase, and for the rest of his life, he saw that increase come to him.

In Genesis 17, God again spoke to Abram regarding His covenant with him, changed his name from Abram to Abraham, established the way the covenant was to work and declared that He would "multiply [him] exceedingly." God would continue to increase Abraham in land, cattle, descendants and wealth. God caused him to prosper in all aspects of his life.

When you grasp this relationship between God and Abraham, you can begin to better see *your* relationship with God today because we are the "seed of Abraham." Galatians 3:29 says, "And if you are Christ's, then you are Abraham's seed, and heirs according to the promise." Therefore, the better you know how God blessed Abraham, the better you will understand your own position in Him.

Blessing or Materialism?

For too long, the Body of Christ has struggled with the realization that God wants to bring increase and even financial miracles into our lives. There seems to have been an underlying fear that to want God to bring any kind of material increase was to be *materialistic*. This fear of financial increase as a part of the blessing of God has been fed by people who have a misconception of God Himself.

To be materialistic means *to endeavor to satisfy an emotional or spiritual need with a physical thing.* No believer wants to have material things in a place of priority over God. Material increase is fine as long as *you have* the things you possess, but *they* do not *have* you.

When King David fell to his darkest moment through adultery and murder, God spoke to him and said,

"...I anointed you king over

Israel, and I delivered you from the hand of Saul. I gave you your master's house and your master's wives into your keeping, and gave you the house of Israel and Judah. And if that had been too little, I also would have given you much more!" (2 Samuel 12:7-8).

God did not rebuke David by telling him he had too much. God said He would have given David even more if he had wanted more. David had sinned, but it was not the wealth or power that was the problem. God was ready and willing to increase him even further if David had wanted it. God does not want to withhold His abundance from you, but you must walk with Him and honor His Word for the promise of increase to come to you.

The Miracle of Abundance

In understanding the attitude God demonstrates regarding abundance, you see in the very first miracle Jesus performed that it was a miracle of abundance. It was during a wedding feast in Cana, and the host had run out of wine to serve his guests. Jesus' mother told Him of the problem and then instructed the servants of the host by saying, "Whatever He says to you, do it" (John 2:5). Verse 11 further states, "This beginning of signs Jesus did in Cana of Galilee, and manifested His glory; and His disciples believed in Him."

Jesus' glory was revealed through a miracle that did not heal anyone nor did it deliver anyone from demonic power. It was a miracle of abundance. Jesus did what He saw

His Father do, He provided abundant supply—*increase!*

It *is* significant that the first miracle was a miracle of abundance. God has made a clear case that blessing and increase are in His plan for His people.

Just as Abraham believed those first words that God would bless him through His covenant, you also must receive His promise and His plan by faith and activate it in your life.

To Establish His Covenant

Look closely again at Psalm 115:16: "The heaven, even the heavens, are the Lord's; but the earth He has given to the children of men."

The wealth of the earth is not for

those who are living for greed or lust or selfishness. It is for those who walk with God and have put Him first in their life. The world has misused wealth and its power for ungodly or personal gain, and not the purpose for which God gave it. Wealth and riches are given to us for the purpose of establishing the covenant of God. Deuteronomy 8:18 says,

> And you shall remember the Lord your God, for it is He who gives you power to get wealth, that He may establish His covenant which He swore to your fathers, as it is this day.

God gives you the power to get wealth. His wisdom and anointing empower you to possess the wealth and riches for the purpose of establishing—*to set up, ordain or to prove*—His covenant.

God made a covenant with Abraham and established it again with Isaac and Jacob. In that covenant, He promised to bless and multiply them and their seed. He is bound to His Word, and therefore He is bound to bring that increase into your life if you will walk by faith with Him.

It is time for the increase of the people of God to be, "exceedingly abundantly above all that we ask or think" (Ephesians 3:20). It is the day for increase to come and the message of faith in God to flourish.

As you increase, you are able to use that wealth to further establish God's covenant in others. The ultimate plan for your increase is in order that the message and power of His covenant may be brought to all people—worldwide.

Lay hold on your covenant, and God will establish His covenant of increase in you.

Chapter 3

The Seeds of Your Increase Are in Your Hand

To the world, God's plan for our increase seems upside down. In His plan, you give in order to receive. The way up with God is down because the seeds of your increase are in your hand.

Harvest—it's the reason for everything the successful farmer does. The plowing, the sowing, the fertilizing, the spraying is all for the harvest. Every second of preparation and every drop of sweat is focused on one goal—to get the maximum harvest possible from the ground into which he sows.

God's Word tells us we should see life much like we see that farm and that we should see our part in making life productive and successful like the actions of the farmer. The principle that the farmer uses to make his farm-land productive is the same basic principle on which all of God's king-dom operates. The principle of seed-time and harvest is foundational to the working of the kingdom of God. It's how His kingdom operates.

The importance of this great truth is clearly stated in Galatians 6:7, "A man's harvest in life will depend entirely on what he sows" *(Phillips Translation)*. This means that the results you experience in life—the growth, advancement, increase or loss—are a result of the seeds you sow.

Nothing you experience in life is exempt from this basic truth. Your present situation is largely a product of the seeds you have sown in the past. The good news is your future can be changed by the seeds you sow today. Your future is in your hand and in your heart in seed form. If you can learn to plant the seeds that will create the kind of life that God has destined you to live in, you will find His plan becoming a reality for you.

A Law That Has Never Changed

This law of the kingdom has been from the beginning. In Genesis 8:22, we see that God has declared this law will remain for all of time: "While the earth remains, seedtime and harvest, cold and heat, winter and summer, and day and night shall not cease."

Planting seeds and creating a harvest is the way God established for the earth to be sustained and continue to increase. All of life is made up of sowing and reaping. If you will sow the kind of seeds that will produce what you want in life, your reaping will be a joy. This is the system, you sow and your seeds will grow.

The person who will see increase is the one who grasps this law and develops an attitude just like the farmer. The farmer knows that reaping comes only because he sows the seeds for harvest. Second Timothy 2:6 says, "The hard working farmer must be first to partake of the crops."

God is a God of increase. Just as

He made the universe to continue to expand and the earth to continue to replenish itself, He made His entire kingdom in heaven and on earth to bring continual increase. It is His design. It is important to understand that God's way is to create increase.

Like the farmer in His field, you are to create increase. Then you are to be the first to grow from the increase that comes. God expects that His Word will bring increase to you. He wants you to be a source of strength and help to others. But if you have not received for yourself, it is going to be hard for you to help anyone else.

You must decide to increase in His plan. He said in Psalm 115:14, "May the Lord give you increase more and more, you and your children." It is His desire for all that you set your hand to do to grow and be blessed.

Your Increase Is in Your Hands

To participate in God's plan for increase, we must understand that it does not come the way the world thinks it should. We see this in the life of Jesus.

Jesus Himself was the Seed that would be sown to create a harvest of deliverance for all of mankind. He said,

> The hour has come that the Son of Man should be glorified. Most assuredly, I say to you, unless a grain of wheat falls into the ground and dies, it remains alone; but if it dies, it produces much grain (John 12:23-24).

His life was to be a seed that dies in the ground, but the result would be His life multiplied in people. Jesus went on to say how we would experience the same thing,

> He who loves his life will lose it, and he who hates his life in this world will keep it for eternal life. If anyone serves Me, let him follow Me; and where I am, there My servant will be also. If anyone serves Me, him My Father will honor (verses 25-26).

John the Baptist said, "He must increase, but I must decrease" (John 3:30). To the world, this way of thinking looks upside down. That is not a natural way of thinking, but it is the way God works. The way up with God is first down. Increase is a result of what you give not what you get.

The Way to Increase with God
Is to Decrease

For your life to multiply, you must let go of your own life and sow it into His life. When you die to yourself, you will find that His life will now rise up in you. Your life is now His eternal, supernatural life. Then, the new life of God will be flowing within you. Philippians 2:5-11 describes this further:

> Let this mind be in you which was also in Christ Jesus, who, being in the form of God, did not consider it robbery to be equal with God, but made Himself of no reputation, taking the form of a bondservant, and coming in the likeness of

men. And being found in appearance as a man, He humbled Himself and became obedient to the point of death, even the death of the cross. Therefore God also has highly exalted Him and given Him the name which is above every name, that at the name of Jesus every knee should bow, of those in heaven, and of those on earth, and of those under the earth, and that every tongue should confess that Jesus Christ is Lord, to the glory of God the Father.

Jesus first became as a man and let go of His position and reputation. He did not consider His equality with God a thing to cling to but became a bondservant. As the result of letting go, He was given a Name that is above every name.

You do not need to fear that God is going to degrade you or crush you. He is always working to lift you and build your life into something wonderful. However, it will always mean you will have to embrace His way—letting go of the way your flesh or reasoning works. This is the way to godly increase. You sow the seeds, and God brings the increase. Then you reap the harvest and enjoy the fruit. Now you have something to give to others.

Reaping More Than Just Miracles

Too often, people are looking to God for the wrong thing. People love miracles, and I do too. Yet we are not to live for miracles. Miracles are a result of a crisis. When people do not live by the laws of God and a crisis comes, they have God's Word that He is on their side and wants to deliver them.

We are not limited to living from crisis to crisis. We are to live by the fruit we produce. Remember: *Increase is a result of seedtime and harvest.* God's Word is His will in seed form. In any area of life in which we need a harvest, we need only to plant the seeds of His promise. Healing, peace, love and joy are just some of the results that are increased by sowing the seeds of God's Word.

Anything we have can become a seed that we sow. If we need love, we sow love. If we need joy, we plant joy. If we need peace, we need to be peace makers. The principle is clear: God has given us the tools to receive any harvest we need. Begin by planting a seed.

Your Increase Is in Your Hands

One of our greatest tools for sowing and harvesting is our financial giving. Think about what money really is. It is a person's life in seed form. We give of our time and labor or ideas to gain our money. Now, through our money, we can sow our lives into many areas of the kingdom.

When we sow for promoting the Word, we are setting increase in motion. Giving in this way is a spiritual thing which God receives and multiplies. When we give, our money leaves our hands, but it never leaves our lives. It leaves our present situation, and it enters our future. God can add to what you have, but He can multiply what you give.

Jesus demonstrated this one day

as He was teaching and healing a multitude of people. They had been ministering into the evening and the people were hungry. Notice what He did:

> When it was evening, His disciples came to Him, saying, "This is a deserted place, and the hour is already late. Send the multitudes away, that they may go into the villages and buy themselves food." But Jesus said to them, "They do not need to go away. You give them something to eat," and they said to Him, "We have here only five loaves and two fish." He said, "Bring them here to Me." Then He commanded the multitudes to sit down on the grass. And He took the five loaves and the

two fish, and looking up to heaven, He blessed and broke and gave the loaves to the disciples; and the disciples gave to the multitudes. So they all ate and were filled, and they took up twelve baskets full of the fragments that remained (Matthew 14:15-20).

Jesus told the disciples to take what they had and give it to Him. What they had in their hands was actually food that belonged to a young man present. Jesus blessed what they gave Him and gave it back to them. But now there was a difference.

Once again, the disciples had in their hands the loaves and fish, only this time it was blessed and able to be multiplied. The disciples began giving the food to the people until everyone was full. They went from not having enough to having more than enough. And they did it by following one simple instruction. Jesus said, "Bring them here to Me." If what you have in your hands does not meet your need—it may be your seed.

Give God Something to Work With

The disciples did not have enough to meet the need, so Jesus said to give what they had to Him. He has established the laws of His kingdom to bring you into a place of abundant supply, but you must put something in His hands.

This miracle supply happened right before their eyes. That is not always the way increase comes, but increase always comes. Galatians 6:9

says, "And let us not grow weary while doing good, for in due season we shall reap if we do not lose heart." You must not give up but continue to sow and expect the harvest. Due season *always* comes!

Your increase is in your hands in seed form. Plant what you have and watch it grow.

Chapter 4

Reaping in the Days of Abundant Harvest

The harvest is crying out; the reaper is crying out. Something is about to change for those who understand the rules for reaping. The Body of Christ is getting ready to step into the greatest aspects of reaping it has ever known. The most abundant harvest the world has seen is in the fields right now. It is time for us to lay claim to the "due season" to which Galatians 6:9 refers: "And let us not grow weary while doing good, for in due season we shall reap if we do not lose heart."

This is the time we can discover how to reap all that we have sown and see the multiplying impact of God's laws for harvest. It is time to put in the sickle and reap abundantly.

But first we must understand what this harvest is all about. The biblical principle of harvest primarily refers to people being born again— entering a relationship with Jesus Christ and being delivered from the power of sin. The ultimate goal of ministry is for people to know Jesus and become His disciples.

There are other aspects of harvesting that each believer must grow in personally to become a more effective part of the harvest of people for the kingdom of God. In this last-days harvest, those who reap will be those who understand the rules for reaping.

You Were Made to Reap

One of the basic conditions for reaping is that we sow. We sow seeds of time, love, money, spiritual truth and other things. The problem I find is that many times people are sowing their seeds of faith through their offerings or tithes, but they are not reaping. To see the increase God has provided become a reality, we must allow the same Word that stirs us up to sow also stir us up to reap.

We must understand how to sow in faith and reap in faith as well. God said in Proverbs 8:21 that He has given us His wisdom, "That I may cause those who love me to inherit wealth, that I may fill their treasuries." God's desire is clear; He wants us to increase in wealth. His way to our increase is through His wisdom, and His way to wisdom is through His Word. His Word is His wisdom. By walking in it, we find the wisdom to bring wealth and increase into our lives.

Let God's Word Show You What Is Yours

According to His Word, we are to reap things from which we have been defrauded—things withheld from our possession. James 5:1-4 gives an open rebuke to those who are rich but whose priorities are ungodly:

> Come now, you rich, weep and howl for your miseries that are coming upon you! Your riches are corrupted, and your garments are moth-eaten. Your gold and silver are corroded, and their corrosion will be a

witness against you and will eat your flesh like fire. You have heaped up treasure in the last days. Indeed the wages of the laborers who mowed your fields, which you kept back by fraud, cry out; and the cries of the reapers have reached the ears of the Lord of Sabaoth.

Notice what is crying out here. It is the wages that are not paid. Money cries out! When you have earned wages and are not paid those wages, the money is still yours. Though it is not in your hands, it cries out. It is part of your harvest.

The laws of God recognize as yours what should have come to you but was withheld from you. That money owed you becomes a witness against whoever holds it wrongfully.

Part of your personal harvest is the money and things that have been kept back from you by the kingdom of darkness. The seed you have sown into the kingdom of God that has not seemed to bring any increase is still your seed, and the harvest remains yours. It is time to get your harvest out of the grasp of the enemy and into your hands.

If you have been defrauded, it may feel like you have been beaten. But even the courts of the land are not your final word. You have the high court in heaven and your heavenly Father as the Judge. The money itself is a witness in that court. You can still win and see God restore to you anything that has been defrauded from you.

It Is Time for You to Cry Out

Notice again in verse 4 that not

only were the wages crying out, but also the reapers who had been defrauded were crying out. If you are a sower, you are also a reaper. It is time for the reapers to cry out to receive what belongs to them. It is time for you to receive what belongs to you.

The Amplified Bible says that the rich, "...have heaped together treasure for the last days" (James 5:3). Proverbs 13:22 says, "But the wealth of the sinner is stored up for the righteous." Wealth is made to be handled by the righteous.

I began to apply this to the sowing Vikki and I have done over the years. I realized that as diligent sowers, we are entitled to reap a harvest. We have sown our labor, our money, our love and our lives into the kingdom of

God since 1971. We have seed all over the world and in many different kinds of fields. We are sowers. Yet, our reaping has not been the kind of increase our sowing could produce. We were seeing wonderful growth and increase but not to the degree we knew was available. Remember, Jesus spoke of some receiving thirty, some sixty and some a hundred fold.

Then God began to speak to me of the importance of pressing in to receive the harvest. He stirred me up to look to the fields that I had sown into and to expect a harvest in each of those fields.

Lay Claim to Your Harvest

Harvest does not come out of the field on its own. You must bring the harvest into the barns. When the reapers cry out, something different begins to happen. The seed sown, the wages withheld, the increase due begins to witness to the Father God that harvest must come into the reapers' hands.

Your enemy will steal from you and hold your goods as long as you allow. You are the one who can cry out to the Lord of the harvest and begin to reap where you have sown.

Galatians 6:7 tells us how far-reaching this sowing and reaping can go: "A man's harvest in life will depend entirely on what he sows" *(Phillips Translation)*. Every aspect of life is affected by the seed you sow. You can begin to harvest in every possible area if you will sow, determine to reap and not tolerate your enemy stealing your harvest.

Some do not receive their harvest because they do not sow. You must be a sower to be a reaper. Others do not receive because they leave their increase in the field. You must put in the sickle and reap. There is power released when you make a decision. When you decide to press in and receive your harvest, there is power released through you to receive. Reaping is not automatic. Mark 4:27-29 tells how the sower sows:

And should sleep by night and rise by day, and the seed should sprout and grow, he himself does not know how. For the earth yields crops by itself; first the blade, then the head, after that the full grain in the head. But when the grain ripens, immediately he puts in the sickle, because the harvest has come.

You may not know how God is causing your harvest to come. He makes your seed grow, but you put in the sickle. You are to lay claim to your harvest with the words of your mouth. Declare that it is yours. You have sown the seeds, and the harvest is yours for the reaping. Stir yourself up to receive it.

Seed you have sown or offerings you have given that have not seemed to bring what God's Word has promised could be held back fraudulently by your enemy. That harvest is crying out as James 5:4 states. Your seed is to bring a harvest into your hands. The harvest is made to be handled by you.

When the reaper of the harvest

cries out and the harvest itself is crying out, something is about to change! To cry out to God is not to beg or complain to Him but rather to appropriate His Word and receive His promises by faith. You simply declare that His promises are true and the harvest is yours now. You decree, "I am a reaper of the promises of God."

Reap Where Others Have Labored

We are to cry out not only for what we have sown but also for what others have sown before us. Notice John 4:38: "I sent you to reap that for which you have not labored; others have labored, and you have entered into their labors." In the covenant of increase God has made through Jesus, we are to reap beyond the seed we have sown and reap where others have labored.

What does it mean to reap where others have labored? Throughout history there have been men and women of God who have sown their offerings, their time, their families and even their own lives for the gospel. Multitudes have traveled to foreign lands to bring the message of Jesus and have never seen the kind of reaping personally or in revival that their sowing should have produced.

There were faithful people who did not see the reality of their harvest, yet they sowed in hope and in faith. While fulfilling the dreams God had placed in their hearts, they gave but did not receive in this life. Their reward in heaven is a great reward, but the seed sown in the earth has not been harvested. The enemy kept them from receiving, but their labor was not lost. The eternal nature of spiritually sown seed continues to wait for someone to reap. The seed they have sown is still alive. Now, Jesus has sent you and me to enter by faith into their labor and reap where they have sown.

Stepping into Your Abundant Harvest

In Deuteronomy 6:10-11, Israel is told that God will bring them into the land He swore to Abraham, Isaac and Jacob,

> To give you large and beautiful cities which you did not build, houses full of all good things, which you did not fill, hewn-out wells which you did not dig, vineyards and olive trees which you did not plant.

Again in Joshua 24:13, God refers to this land saying,

> I have given you a land for which you did not labor, and cities which you did not build, and you dwell in them; you eat of the vineyards and olive groves which you did not plant.

The land of promise was full of blessings which they did not earn but had to pursue and receive. The picture we have of Israel entering the promise is ours also. God provided a land of milk and honey for Israel, but they had to go in and possess it.

Faith begins where the will of God is understood. Your faith can rise up above the realm you have lived in until now. You can become a reaper who is receiving more than thirty or sixty times and step into receiving more than a hundred times.

It is not time to stop or even slow down in your giving and sowing. It is time to set your faith higher and let your giving reflect the faith in your heart. Then set your heart to reap, and watch the days of abundant harvest come to you.

References

The Amplified Bible. © 1954, 1958 by the Lockman Foundation, La Habra, California.

The New Testament in Modern English. J.B. Phillips © 1958 by the MacMillan Company, New York.

New King James Version. © 1982 by Thomas Nelson, Inc. Nashville, Tennessee.

New Testament in Modern Speech. Richard Francis Weymouth © 1978 by Kregel Publications, Grand Rapids, Michigan.

At the heart of Dennis Burke Ministries is the compelling desire to see lives changed—healed, restored, and renewed by the power of the Word of God. Dennis and Vikki Burke are a dynamic ministry team who have brought life to the Body of Christ.

They have traveled internationally sharing answers and bringing freedom to various parts of the world from Australia to Ukraine, Japan to Malaysia and throughout the United States.

After more than 20 years of ministry, they have stepped into one of the dreams they have held in their hearts—the *Fresh Fire* television broadcast. Their dedication has affected thousands as they are impacting God's people with the love of God.

Books Authored by Dennis Burke

You Can Conquer Life's Conflicts
Knowing God Intimately
The Rewards of the Diligent
The Law of the Wise
*How to Meditate God's Word
Yielding to the Holy Spirit
Grace—Power Beyond Your Ability

*Available in Spanish

Books Authored by Vikki Burke

Aim Your Child Like an Arrow
Relief and Refreshing

A complete catalog of books, audio and video
tapes is available by writing:

Dennis Burke Ministries
P. O. Box 150043
Arlington, TX 76015
(817) 277-9627
or call 1-800-742-4050
for credit card orders only.

*Please include your prayer requests
when you write.*

Visit our web site at
www.dennisburkeministries.org or
e-mail us at *Dbmin@aol.com*